W9-BIC-582

THE
GREEKS

Susan Williams

Thomson Learning • New York

Look into the Past

First published in the
United States in 1993 by
Thomson Learning
115 Fifth Avenue
New York, NY 10003

First published in 1993 by
Wayland (Publishers) Ltd
61 Western Road, Hove
East Sussex, BN3 1JD, England

Copyright © 1993 Wayland (Publishers) Ltd

U.S. revision copyright © 1993 Thomson Learning

Cataloging-in-Publication Data applied for.

ISBN: 1-56847-059-2

Printed in Italy.

Picture acknowledgments

The publishers wish to thank the following for providing the photographs for this book: reproduced by courtesy of the Trustees of British Museum 7 (right), 9 (bottom), 16; C. M. Dixon 10, 11 (right), 14 (top), 20, 23 (top), 27 (top), 28; E. T. Archive 29 (top); Werner Forman Archive cover, 17 (below left), 18; Michael Holford cover, 5 (bottom), 7 (left, British Museum), 8 (British Museum), 9 (top, British Museum), 11 (left, British Museum), 12 (Gerry Clyde), 15 (British Museum), 17 (top and bottom right, British Museum), 19 (both; right, British Museum), 21 (both, British Museum), 24, 25 (both; top, British Museum), 26 (British Museum), 27 (bottom), 29 (bottom, British Museum); Mansell Collection 13 (both), 14 (bottom), 22.

CONTENTS

Words that apear in **bold italic** in the text are explained in the glossary on page 30.

WHO WERE THE ANCIENT GREEKS?

The customs and way of life of the *ancient* Greeks, who lived more than 2,500 years ago, have affected our lives today. The politics, language, literature, art, and sports of many countries all show links with the Greek *civilization* in some way. So the more we know about the history of Greece, the more we understand about how we live today.

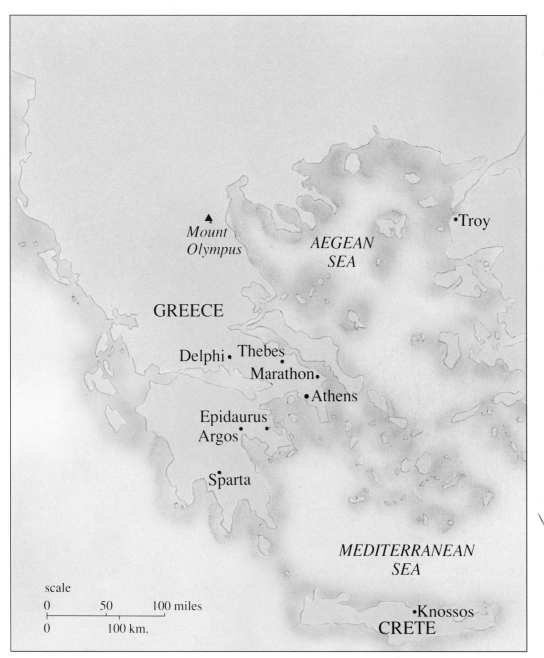

Mount Olympus

AEGEAN SEA

•Troy

GREECE

Delphi• •Thebes

Marathon•

•Athens

Epidaurus

Argos

Sparta

MEDITERRANEAN SEA

scale

0   50   100 miles

0   100 km.

•Knossos

CRETE

Archaeologists use remains (called *artifacts*) that have been found in the area that was ancient Greece to discover how people lived hundreds of years ago.

Pictures on ancient pots, vases, and coins show us how the Greeks used to live. The ruins of buildings and the writings of poets, playwrights, and historians also give us information.

One big difference from our modern way of life is that the Greeks had slaves. Another difference is that they believed in many **gods** and **goddesses.** Also, Greek society was organized entirely by men. Women did not take part in public life.

Greece is a land of ▶ mountains. In ancient times, the mountains separated groups of people from each other. This led to the development of separate communities, which were called *city-states.* Athens, Sparta, Argos, and Thebes were four of many city-states.

Today, the different regions of Greece are joined together by such modern inventions as the car and the telephone.

◀ This picture shows the remains of the entrance to the Minoan palace of Knossos. It had over one thousand rooms, which were built around a courtyard in the middle. The palace was built by a group of people called the Minoans 3,500 years ago, in the fifteenth century B.C., on Crete, a large Greek island. When people talk about the greatest period of Greek civilization, they usually mean the fifth century B.C. (2,500 years ago). This is known as the *classical* period, which produced the art, politics, and literature that have been admired for so many years.

THE GREEK LANGUAGE

The word "alphabet" comes from the first two letters of the Greek alphabet: alpha and beta. The English alphabet is similar to the Greek alphabet and many English words are based on Greek words. The word "telephone," for example, is made up of the Greek words for "far off" (tele) and "voice" (phone). The word "hippopotamus" is made up of the words for "horse" (hippos) and "river" (potamos).

▼ Here is the old Greek alphabet. Some of our letters are different. But you could you write your name in Greek letters.

Ancient Greek letter	Name of Greek letter	Nearest English letter
A	alpha	A
B	beta	B
Λ	gamma	G
Δ	delta	D
E	epsilon	E (short)
I	zeta	Z (SD)
H	eta	E (long)
Θ	theta	Th
I	iota	I
K	kappa	K
L	lambda	L
M	mu	M
N	nu	N
XE	xi	X (Ks)
O	omicron	O (short)
Π	pi	P
R	rho	R
E	sigma	S
T	tau	T
V	upsilon	U
Ø	phi	Ph, F
X	khi	Kh, Ch
ØE	psi	PS
Ω	omega	O (long)

This piece of writing tells of **omens** that people believed they could see in the way birds were flying in the sky. The capital letters have been cut into a piece of stone. Perhaps you can tell what some of the letters are.

Most men who lived in Athens were able to read, because boys went to school. They learned literature, music, and physical education. Girls in Athens did not go to school but stayed at home to learn how to look after a family. In Sparta, both girls and boys were taught to read and write.

In this painting on a vase, a man at a festival ▶ in Athens is reciting two long poems written by a blind poet called Homer. Homer's poems are called the *Iliad* and the *Odyssey*. The *Iliad* is about the Trojan War, a war fought between the city-states of Athens and Troy. The *Odyssey* tells the adventures of Odysseus on his travels after the end of the Trojan War.

7

THE CITY-STATE OF ATHENS

The city-state of Athens was very powerful and ruled a large *empire*. It was a rich city because it owned silver mines nearby, where slaves were made to work very hard. The goddess of Athens was Athena and the *emblem* of the city was the owl.

▲ This is a little clay statue of two women talking together. Women in Athens were expected to stay at home and to care for their families. In one famous Greek play, the **heroine** insists that she would prefer to go into battle than to be stuck at home.

This is a bust of ▶
Pericles. He was a
great leader of Athens
in the fifth century B.C.
He had the Parthenon
and other beautiful
temples built, and had
the port of the city,
Piraeus, improved. He
led Athens in the war
against Sparta, which
lasted from 431 B.C. to
404 B.C.

▼ This painting on a vase shows men voting.
The people of Athens first invented the idea of
democracy, which is the Greek word for "rule by
the people." Because Athens was a democracy,
the voters of the city could choose their leaders
and be asked to serve in government.

However, not everyone was able to take
part in elections — women, slaves, and freed
slaves were not allowed to vote. Nowadays,
most western countries are democracies,
in which all adults have the right
to vote for the government
they prefer.

WARLIKE SPARTA

Sparta was a city-state where all the men were full-time soldiers. They could not leave their barracks to live with their families until they reached the age of thirty. If they did something bad they lost their *citizenship;* then they had to wear special clothes and were not allowed to shave. Children in Sparta had to learn to be brave when they were very young. When boys reached the age of seven, they left home to live in *military* barracks. They had only one tunic to wear for a whole year. They had to take part in a flogging contest, during which some boys died. A statue was built to those boys who could bear the pain for the longest time.

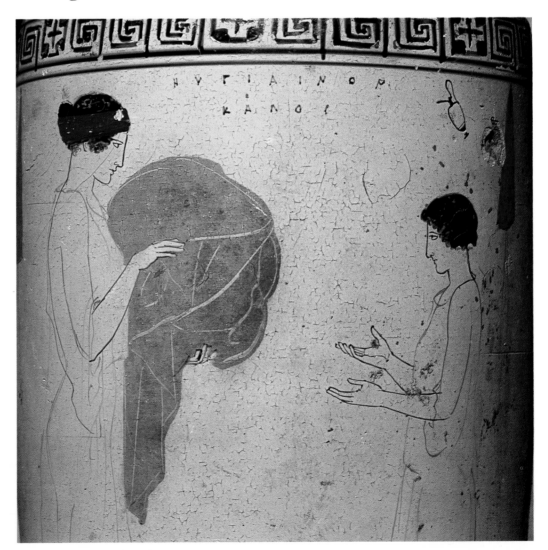

This is a painting ▶ on an oil jar of a woman and her slave. Slaves in Sparta were owned by the state and were called **helots.** They did most of the work that had to be done and were treated very badly.

This Spartan girl athlete is wearing a short tunic, so that she can run freely. Girls in Sparta were encouraged to exercise and grew up with more freedom than girls in Athens. Women mixed with men and could own land. But they could not vote or hold any positions of power.

▲ This sculpture of Leonidas, a brave Spartan king, was found near his tomb on the *acropolis,* the highest point in the city of Sparta.

HOMES AND BUILDINGS

Greek houses were built with sun-dried bricks and wood and were arranged around an open courtyard. Women and children lived separately from the men in their families. The men lived in the more public areas, where visitors were made welcome. A stranger was not supposed to enter a room containing women, unless he had been invited to do so by the man of the house.

◀ This is a drain at the Minoan palace of Knossos, on the island of Crete, built about 3,500 years ago. The Minoans built an efficient water system to supply water to the palace and to drain it away. The queen even had running water in her bathroom and a toilet that flushed.

▲ Public buildings were very fine and built of stone and marble. Many were temples to gods and goddesses. This is the Parthenon in Athens. It was built in the classical period and dedicated to Athena, the goddess of the city.

Over 2,000 years later Greek temples were copied in many parts of the world. Many of the government buildings in Washington D.C., for example, have columns like those of the temples of ancient Greece.

◄ This is the porch of the Erechtheion, a temple that was built on the acropolis of Athens, just after the Parthenon. These statues of women take the place of ordinary columns in holding up the roof.

SHOPPING AND EATING

When the Greeks went shopping, they usually took a slave with them to carry what they bought. Shopping was done in the marketplace, which was called the *agora*. People enjoyed meeting each other at the market and chatting together while they chose what to buy.

The ancient Greeks used money to buy food and clothes, just as we do. Their coins, like the one in this picture, were made of gold or silver or a mixture of both. The drachma and the obol were the most common coins. In Athens one drachma was worth six obols. A loaf of bread cost one obol and the average price of a slave was 150 drachmae.

◀ These storage jars were kept at the palace of Knossos. Wine, oil, and grain were stored in jars and cool rooms. The ancient Greeks did not have refrigerators, so it was difficult to keep food fresh during the long, hot summers.

▲ This vase-painting shows a banquet, where men are drinking wine and relaxing. Women were not usually invited to these special occasions. The food eaten in ancient Greece was simple: bread, cereal, fruit, vegetables, eggs, milk, cheese, and fish. Meat was not eaten very often. Honey was used to sweeten food. The Greeks loved garlic – the Athenians were very disappointed when they could not obtain garlic during the war against Sparta.

15

WHAT PEOPLE WORE

To stay cool in summer, the ancient Greeks wore light and comfortable clothes. Both women and men wore a *chiton,* which was a tunic made from a rectangular piece of cloth. Women wore long ones to their feet. Men wore them short, to their knees. They also wore cloaks, hats, and shoes or sandals. Women wore a shawl called a *peplos.* Every year a peplos was woven for the statue of the goddess Athena and was carried in procession to her temple in Athens.

This is a vase-painting of Hermes, the messenger-god. He is wearing winged boots so that he can fly. His other clothes, such as the broadbrimmed hat, are like the clothes worn by ordinary *mortals* when they were traveling.

In this bedroom scene, which is painted on a vase, the young woman who is sitting is being dressed for her wedding. There is a mirror on the wall and another woman is holding a trinket box for her to look inside. She is choosing jewelry to wear at her marriage.

The Greeks made lovely jewelry in gold and silver, which was worn by women. This is a spiral bracelet, made of gold.

This necklace has ▶ been carved from gold. Some of the beads are shaped like heads.

17

RELIGIOUS BELIEFS

The Greeks believed that there were many goddesses and gods. They made *sacrifices* to them in temples, believing that this would bring them good fortune. The gods behaved just like humans, having fun and getting cross with each other. They were different from humans, though, because they had *supernatural* powers and controlled nature and the lives of people. The king of the gods was Zeus, who controlled the weather.

◀ This is a photograph of Mount Olympus, a high mountain in Greece. The peak of Mount Olympus was the home of all the gods and goddesses, except Hades, the king of the underworld, and Dionysus, the god of wine and dancing.

This is a bronze ▶ head of Aphrodite, who was the Greek goddess of love and beauty. Although the bronze is damaged because it is so old, it gives us some idea of how the Greeks thought a beautiful woman should look.

◀ This temple of Apollo, the god of the sun, is at Delphi. In order to receive messages from the gods, people would visit an *oracle.* They would go to a temple with a question for a god to answer. The most important oracle was that of Apollo at Delphi. The priestess of Apollo delivered the answers, which were written down by the priests.

GREEK MYTHS

Many stories were told about the gods and goddesses and about the way in which they organized the lives of ordinary women and men. Tales were also told about *heroes,* who were brave and good-looking. Heroes were of *noble* birth and one of their parents was often a god or a goddess. The hero named Achilles, for instance, was the son of a king and a sea nymph. Stories like these, about the world of the supernatural, are called myths.

▼ This sculpture on a tomb shows the hero Oedipus killing the Sphinx, a monster that was partly a winged lion and partly a woman. By a tragic mistake, Oedipus killed his father and married his mother. He was so horrified when he learned the truth that he blinded himself.

This picture on a ► wine jar shows Odysseus and his men sailing past the island of creatures called the Sirens. The Sirens had the bodies of birds and the heads and voices of women. They sang very sweetly in order to attract the sailors to the island, where the rocks would wreck their ships and kill them. Odysseus blocked the ears of his men with wax and had himself tied to the mast of his ship, so that they would not be tempted to go to the island. In this way they were able to pass the Sirens safely.

This is the hero ▶ Theseus killing the Minotaur, a monster with the body of a man and the head of a bull. The picture is painted on a vase. According to myths, the Minotaur lived in an underground *maze* on the island of Crete and liked to eat people.

Theseus cleverly took a ball of string with him into the maze, which he unwound as he went along. He found the Minotaur and killed it, then followed the string back so that he could find his way out of the maze.

THE THEATER

The first public performance of a play in Athens took place in the fifth century B.C. Plays soon became very popular and were often performed at festivals. Tragedies were serious plays and had sad endings. Comedies were amusing and had happy endings. A group of dancers and singers called a *chorus* talked about the play as it went along, giving it a broader, deeper meaning.

◀ The actors wore masks like the one worn by this comic actor. Some of the audience would be sitting so far away from the stage that they could not see the expressions on an actor's face. Each mask showed a different emotion very clearly, so that everyone in the audience could see how the characters were feeling. Since women did not perform, men had to play both male and female parts. Many plays were about the gods and their way of dealing with humans.

◀ Like all the theaters built in ancient Greece, the theater at Epidaurus is outdoors. Best preserved of all Greek theaters, it seats some 14,000 people. Because it was cut into a slope, everyone could see the play. It is still in use today.

Plays written in ▶ ancient Greece are still performed today. This Greek tragedy is being acted in a modern theater. The Greeks enjoyed going out to see a play, just as we do.

GREEK THOUGHT AND CULTURE

Greek *philosophers* thought about the best ways to live. The word "philosopher" in Greek means lover of wisdom. Socrates was an Athenian philosopher who tried to understand the nature of goodness. He was put on trial because he encouraged people to question their belief in the gods. He was condemned to die by drinking a poison called hemlock.

▲ The shape and size of Greek temples were pleasing to the eye. This was because the Greeks knew a lot about mathematics and planned their buildings carefully. The mathematician Pythagoras developed ideas that children learn in school today.

This painting on a vase shows Apollo playing the cithara, a type of *lyre*, to the goddesses Hera and Nike. Mortal women and men enjoyed listening and dancing to music, just as the gods did. The Spartans particularly liked military music.

This picture of dolphins was painted on the wall of the queen's room at the palace of Knossos. Many vases, cups, and pots have been found that were painted by the ancient Greeks. They liked pictures of nature, war, sport, and the world of the gods, as well as detailed patterns and decorations.

25

THE OLYMPICS AND SPORT

Every four years the ancient Greeks held a festival of sports called the Olympic Games in honor of the god Zeus. Our own Olympic Games, which began in 1896, are based on the ancient Olympics.

◀ The ancient Greeks liked to be fit and strong and enjoyed exercise. As far as we know, Greek society was the first to take sports seriously. In Athens, boys took part in athletics at school and men spent a lot of time at the gymnasium, where they exercised naked. The boxers painted on this vase are naked, apart from gloves of oxhide laced around their hands.

◀ The Olympic Games were held at Olympia. This photograph shows what is left of the starting line in the stadium. There was also a gymnasium and a *hippodrome* for horse races. Olympic events included foot-races, wrestling, and a chariot race. Only men could take part and there were no team sports. Winners were awarded crowns of wreaths.

Runners tried to ▶ run as fast as possible in the races held at this stadium at Delphi. It is smaller than the stadiums where the Olympic Games are held today.

Our word "marathon," which means a long-distance race, comes from ancient Greece. It is the name of a Greek city where the Athenians won a battle. News of this battle was taken by a fast runner to Athens, about twenty miles away. It is much easier today to use tele-phones and fax machines to deliver urgent messages.

27

THE GREEKS AT WAR

The Greeks were often at war. In the fifth century B.C., the city-states fought together to defeat the Persians, who were trying to conquer them. Then Athens and Sparta fought a war against each other, which Sparta won. In the next century, the Greeks were conquered by King Philip of Macedonia.

This detail on a ▶ vase shows the wooden horse of Troy. In his poem the *Iliad*, Homer wrote that the Greeks used a wooden horse to trick the Trojans during the Trojan War.

The war began because a Trojan prince took Helen, the Queen of Argos, back to his city. The Greeks were furious and went to Troy to get her back. After ten years of war, they hid soldiers inside a wooden horse and left it outside the walls of Troy. The Trojans thought it was a gift and took it into their city. Greek soldiers climbed out of the horse, waving their spears. They gave the Trojans a terrible surprise and defeated them.

◀ The figure in this cup is that of a **hoplite,** a heavily-armed foot soldier. Spartan hoplites were the most feared, because they were so well trained. Each city-state had its own army and navy. Athens was proud of its powerful navy, which used warships called *triremes.*

As we have seen in the preceding pages, the civilization of ancient Greece was similar to our own. Our politics, language, literature, arts, and sports have grown from those of ancient Greece.

Greek soldiers did ▶ not have guns, but fought with spears, swords, and bows and arrows. This bronze helmet would have helped to protect a soldier's head from the spears of his enemy.

29

GLOSSARY

Acropolis   The highest point of a Greek city, which was strongly defended.

Agora   Greek marketplace.

Ancient   Belonging to a time long ago.

Archaeologists   People who study objects and remains from ancient times.

Artifacts   Objects made by people, such as tools or pots, that archaeologists study to find out how people used to live.

Barracks   A building where soldiers live.

Chiton   A tunic worn by ancient Greeks.

Chorus   A group of singers and dancers who comment on a play.

Citizenship   The rights and duties of a member of a community.

City-state   A city that rules itself, as if it is a small country.

Civilization   A particular group of people and their way of life.

Classical   The period of Greek civilization in the fifth century B.C. The word is used generally when talking about ancient Greek or Roman civilizations.

Democracy   A form of society where people can vote for their choice of leader; government by the people.

Emblem   An object that stands for something else.

Empire   A large group of countries governed by one nation.

God   A male superhuman being with power over nature and human beings.

Goddess   A female superhuman being with power over nature and human beings.

Helots   What slaves in Sparta were called.

Heroes   Men who were admired for their great deeds and goodness, and were often the main characters in plays or poems. Similar women characters were called *heroines.*

Hippodrome   An arena for chariot races.

Hoplites   Heavily-armed foot soldiers.

Lyre   A musical instrument made from a tortoise shell. Strings were plucked to make music to accompany songs.

Marathon   A long-distance race; also a city in ancient Greece.

Maze   A confusing network of passages.

Military   To do with soldiers and war.

Mortals   Beings that will eventually die.

Noble   Belonging to the highest class of society.

Omens   Signs of the future, of things that will happen.

Oracle   A place where gods and goddesses were asked for advice or information about the future.

Peplos   A shawl worn by Greek women.

Philosophers   People who use reason to try to understand the nature of truth and the best way of living in society.

Sacrifices   Killing people or animals to offer to a god or goddess.

Supernatural   Beyond the ordinary forces of nature.

Temple   A building for the worship of goddesses and gods.

Trireme   A Greek warship with three levels of oars.

IMPORTANT DATES

These events occurred so long ago that historians cannot always be sure of exact years.

3000-1100 B.C. Minoan civilization on Crete; Knossos palace built during this time

1600-1200 B.C. Mycenean civilization

1193 B.C. Destruction of Troy by the Greeks

776 B.C. First Olympic Games

750 B.C. onwards Greek city-states emerge

534 B.C. First performance of drama in Athens

490 B.C. Battle of Marathon

479 B.C. Persian invasion of Greece defeated

478 B.C. onwards Classical period of Greek civilization, when democracy, the arts, and philosophy flowered

431 B.C. War between Athens and Sparta begins

404 B.C. Defeat of Athens by Sparta

399 B.C. Trial and execution of Socrates

358 B.C. Theater at Epidaurus built

338 B.C. The Greeks are conquered by Macedonia (now northern Greece)

BOOKS TO READ

Bains, Rae. *Ancient Greece.* Mahwah, NJ: Troll Associates, 1985

Crosher, Judith. *The Greeks.* Needham Heights, MA: Silver, Burdett & Ginn, 1985

Horton, Casey. *Ancient Greeks,* Revised Edition. New York: Gloucester Press, 1984

Odijk, Pamela. *The Greeks.* Englewood Cliffs, NJ: Silver Burdett Press, 1989

Miquel, Pierre. *Life in Ancient Greece.* Needham Heights, MA: Silver, Burdett & Ginn, 1986

Powell, Anton. *The Greek World.* New York: Warwick Press, 1987

Powell, Anton. *Greece, 1600-30 B.C.* New York: Watts, 1987

Rutland, Jonathon. *See Inside an Ancient Greek Town.* Revised Edition
    New York: Warwick Press, 1986

Starr, Chester G. *Ancient Greeks.* New York: Oxford University Press, 1971

Steel, Barry. *Greek Cities.* New York: The Bookwright Press, 1990

INDEX